D1238105

A Tribute to
THE YOUNG AT HEART

MICHAEL LANDON

By: Jill C. Wheeler

Published by Abdo & Daughters, 6535 Cecilia Circle, Edina, Minnesota 55439.

Library bound edition distributed by Rockbottom Books, Pentagon Tower, P.O. Box 36036, Minneapolis, Minnesota 55435.

Printed in the United States.

Cover Photo: FPG
Inside Photos: UPI / Bettmann 4, 18, 21, 23, 25, 31 & 32
                 FPF 14 & 16

Edited by Rosemary Wallner

LIBRARY OF CONGRESS CATALOGING-IN-PUBLICATION DATA

Wheeler, Jill C., 1964-
   Michael Landon / written by Jill C. Wheeler; [edited by Rosemary Wallner].
      p. cm. -- (The Young at Heart)
   Summary: A look at the life and career of Michael Landon, who believed television could make life better for everyone, as evidenced by creation of the show "Highway to Heaven."
   ISBN 1-56239-113-5 (lib. bdg.)
   1. Landon, Michael, 1937-1991 --Juvenile literature. 2. Television actors and actresses -- United States -- Biography -- Juvenile literature. [1. Landon, Michael, 1937-1991 . 2. Actors and actresses.] I. Wallner, Rosemary, 1964- . II. Title. III. Series: Wheeler, Jill C., 1964- Young at Heart.
PN2287.L2814W48 1992   791.45'028'092--dc20   92-16571
                  [B]

International Standard Book Number:
1-56239-113-5

Library of Congress Catalog Card Number:
92-16571

TABLE OF CONTENTS

A young Michael Landon.

THERE IS SOMETHING GOOD ON TV

How many times have your parents turned off the television while you were watching it? Maybe they say it's because there's nothing good on television.

Most parents take an interest in what programs their children see. They want to make sure their children learn what they should. Yet many television programs are full of violence. The people who make those shows say violence makes the programs exciting.

Michael Landon was different. He did not believe in violence on TV. He believed in television programs that taught right from wrong. He vowed not to work on any show unless he would be comfortable if his children were to watch it.

During more than 30 years in Hollywood, Landon kept his vow. He starred in one hit show after another. He wrote screenplays, directed shows and produced them. He refused to let violence become the theme of his shows. He kept a special place in his heart for the children on his shows and his youthful fans.

Landon said his unhappy childhood made him determined to make life better for other children. He did just that with his imagination, his drive and a wonderful sense of humor.

ANOTHER SHOW BUSINESS FAMILY

Like many actors, Landon's parents had show business careers. His father, Eli Orowitz, publicized movies for RKO Radio Pictures. His mother, Peggy O'Neill, was a Broadway actress in New York.

The couple's first child was a daughter, Evelyn. Then, on Halloween night 1936, they had a son. They named him Eugene Maurice Orowitz. Eugene later would change his name to Michael Landon.

As Eugene grew, he realized his parents were not happy. His father lost his job with the movie studio. He got a new job managing a chain of movie theaters, which made him work long into the night. "By the time he got up in the morning, I was already off to school," Landon recalled. "I saw my father for perhaps an hour at the dinner table."

Eugene's mother was unhappy, too. Eli was Jewish and Peggy had been Catholic. When they married, Peggy gave up her religion. Now she regretted it. Sometimes she missed being an actress. Peggy tried to take her own life more than once.

Peggy and Eli would go for weeks without speaking to each other. Peggy would say to Eugene, "Tell your father dinner is ready," even when Eli was in the room. Then, Eli would say to Eugene, "Tell her I know." Eugene used to pray that his parents would like each other.

ALONE & LONELY

Eugene often went off by himself to escape the battles in his home. By this time, his family had moved to New Jersey to be closer to Eli's work. "In the summertime, I'd go fishing from sunrise to sunset," Landon said. "Or I'd hitchhike to Philadelphia, where I'd sleep for the weekend in a farmhouse."

Other times, Eugene would retreat to a cave near his home. He began stealing cans of food from home and putting them in the cave. Someday he hoped to leave home and live in the cave.

In school, Eugene got good grades but he was not popular. He was one of the few Jewish children in his school. He also had a terrible secret – he often wet his bed at night. His mother would hang the wet sheets out of his window to dry during the day. Eugene would race home from school to take the sheets out of the window. He was afraid his classmates would see them and tease him about his problem.

Eventually, Eugene outgrew his problem. He entered high school and found more friends. He also found he had a very special talent. He tried out for the school track team and discovered he could throw a javelin farther than anyone else. (A javelin is like a spear.)

SPEARING A FUTURE

Eugene's life changed almost overnight. He began to live and breathe the javelin. His coaches told him he might be able to throw the javelin in the Olympics. His grades slipped as he spent more and more time practicing the javelin. But he did not mind. Throwing the javelin was the most important thing to him.

"I wasn't popular in grade school because I was a straight-A student," Landon said. "So when I got to high school, I decided that since I didn't think I was going to college, it would be better if I weren't so smart."

Eugene became one of the best javelin throwers in New Jersey. He surprised many people because he was so small. Sometimes he wondered why he could throw so well. Then one day he saw the movie *Sampson and Delilah*, based on a Bible story. In the story, Sampson has incredible strength because he never cuts his hair. When Delilah secretly cuts Sampson's hair, he loses his strength.

Eugene believed he was like Sampson. He refused to cut his hair. And he continued to throw the javelin farther than his competitors. He kept hoping his father would notice what he was doing. Once Eugene saw his father outside the fence while he was practicing. Eli only watched. He did not come into the stadium. Eugene never forgot that.

If Eli did not notice Eugene's talent, other people did. During his senior year, he threw the javelin more than 211 feet. That was enough to set a national record. A recruiter from the University of Southern California heard about his abilities.

The recruiter saw Eugene throw and told people at USC what he had seen. The school offered Eugene a scholarship. Eugene accepted.

NO FAVORS

Eugene's parents followed their son when he moved to Los Angeles to attend USC. Eli thought he could get a job working for the movies again. Eugene went with him one day to Paramount Studios. Eli knew some of his old friends from RKO now worked at Paramount.

Eugene waited outside the studio gates while his father talked to the guard. Eli returned thirty minutes later. No one had remembered him, and Eli hadn't even made it past the guard.

Eugene never forgot how hurt his father was. The event also changed him. "I wasn't going to owe any-body a favor," he said. "And I didn't expect anything from anybody that had to do with business."

Eli was very disappointed. He was afraid to contact other old friends in case they had forgotten him, too.

He took a job managing an old movie theater in downtown Los Angeles.

Meanwhile, Eugene was working hard to fit in at USC. He attended a different USC campus to improve his grades so he could be on the USC track team. Once he made the team, his fellow athletes teased him about his long hair. In 1954, it was fashionable to have very short hair. The other athletes worried Eugene's long hair would give their team a bad image. They suggested he cut it.

Eugene refused. He believed his hair was the source of his ability. One day, several of his teammates pinned him down. Another cut his hair. Eugene was in tears. He ran outside and threw the javelin. It did not go as far as it usually did. He kept throwing and throwing. Eventually he hurt his arm. He never could throw as well again. USC took away his scholarship.

HOLLYWOOD!

Eugene began working at odd jobs to support himself. He worked in a ribbon factory for a while. He worked on a loading dock. One day a co-worker asked Eugene to help with an audition at Warner Bros. movie studio. Eugene went along as a favor. His friend did not get the part, but Warner Bros. asked Eugene to attend their talent school. He could learn acting there.

The school didn't pay any money. So Eugene started a car washing service on the studio parking lot. He made enough money to pay rent and eat while he dreamed of being an actor. He also decided to change his name. He looked in the phone book and decided on Landon. He always had liked the name Michael, so he used that, too.

The new Michael Landon soon met Dodie Fraser. She was a widow with a nine-year-old son. The two became friends and in 1956 they married. Now Landon had a family to support. He earned about $100 a week with his acting. He also worked as a door-to-door salesman for a while.

Landon's first break came in 1957. Hollywood producers realized there was a big market making movies for teenagers. Horror movies were especially popular. Movie producer Herman Cohen decided to make a horror movie for teenagers called *I Was a Teenage Werewolf*. He needed a handsome young star to interest teenage girls. He found his actor in Landon.

Cohen's choice pleased him. In one scene as a werewolf, Landon had to chase a girl through a gym. Cohen recalled, "When he chased that girl, it was as if he were possessed. There were a lot of steel chairs inside the gym, but they didn't slow him down; he flipped them aside as if they were made out out of paper. I still don't know how he did that."

Many people joked about the name of the movie. Yet *I Was a Teenage Werewolf* was a howling success. It also opened doors for Landon to get better roles – including one on a television series which would become one of America's favorites.

Michael Landon, (left) as Little Joe, in Bonanza.

A CAREER BONANZA

Landon took a variety of roles in the next two years. Many were Western shows, which were very popular. It was no surprise when NBC asked him to star in a new western they were producing. The show was about the Cartwright family who lived in Nevada in the late 1800s. The show, *Bonanza*, hit the airwaves in 1959.

Landon was cast to play the family's youngest son, Little Joe. Suddenly, he was making $500 a week. To celebrate, he went to a Chinese restaurant and ate his fill of egg rolls. He also saved most of his pay. In Hollywood, an actor never knows when his show will be canceled.

Bonanza slowly gained in popularity. Almost immediately, Landon became a hit. He and co-star Dan Blocker, who played Little Joe's brother Hoss, became the most popular of the four Cartwrights. They received bags of fan mail each week. Sadly, Landon's father died suddenly as his son was becoming a star.

Lorne Greene

Landon preferred to leave his work at the studio each day. He wanted his family to have as much privacy as possible. He and Dodie bought a house and adopted another son, Josh. Landon also gave more interviews as *Bonanza* became more popular. Many of Landon's fans were surprised to learn their heartthrob had a wife and two sons!

STAR POWER

By 1961 there were Bonanza Booster Clubs around the country. Landon and Blocker, together with fellow Cartwrights Lorne Greene and Pernell Roberts, began making personal appearances around the country. It meant time away from their families, but it also meant more money.

The weekends away from home took their toll. Landon and Dodie divorced in 1962. The following year, Landon married actress and model Lynn Noe. He also adopted her daughter from a previous marriage, Cheryl. Now he had three adopted children. Within a year, he and Lynn had a daughter of their own, Leslie. Finally, Landon felt he had the family love he never had as a child.

Michael Landon, with former wife Lynn.

18

Landon's career blossomed. He earned more responsibility on the *Bonanza* set. He helped write scripts and directed the show in addition to acting in it. He spent time with the crew members to learn how television shows were made. Some crew members thought he was pushy and difficult to work with. Others admired his determination to learn as much as he could about the business.

By the time *Bonanza* was cancelled in fall 1972, Landon had earned his spurs as a TV star. NBC asked him to help develop new TV series and movies. Now a father of six, he looked forward to his next challenge. He decided there was not enough quality family programming on television. He wanted to work on a project that children could enjoy with their parents. In 1974, he had that opportunity.

AMERICA'S FAVORITE LITTLE HOUSE

The *Little House* books by Laura Ingalls Wilder are some of the most-loved books in America. The books deal with the author's experiences as a child. She and her family were pioneers in the Midwest in the 1870s and 1880s.

An NBC producer named Fred Friendly bought the rights to bring the books to television.

Friendly knew it would be difficult to get NBC to air the show. Most television shows relied on action and violence to attract viewers. Friendly needed a big star to draw people to the show. Landon was the perfect choice. He could star as Laura Ingalls' father, Charles. His influence at NBC would help get the show on the air.

Friendly and Landon soon disagreed about the series. Friendly wanted it to be just like the *Little House* books. Landon wanted to explore other topics. "Today the outside influences that help create strong families don't exist anymore," Landon said. "Maybe *Little House* could bring some of them back."

Friendly also discovered Landon had more in mind than acting. He wanted to write, direct and produce episodes, too. Friendly disagreed, but he was powerless. NBC always sided with Landon.

Michael Landon as Charles Ingalls in Little House on the Prairie.

The pilot movie of *Little House on the Prairie* aired in March 1974. Many people watched and enjoyed the show. NBC made plans to add it to their fall line-up. Friendly resigned before *Little House* became a weekly series.

Landon was *Little House's* driving force. He demanded quality. He also made everyone on the set feel like a family. Child actors were especially important to him. He would call a two-hour recess if he felt any of the young actors were tired. Then they would play games until the child felt better. He also planned parties and picnics. The cast learned to be on the lookout for one of Landon's many practical jokes.

Sometimes, Landon would beckon one of the crew members to come talk to him. He'd lean over, open his mouth, and a tiny frog would pop out. Two of the *Little House* children used to tell their friends Landon ate frogs.

Cast of Little House on the Prairie.

BATTLING DRUGS, DIVORCE & DIRECTORS

Landon's life was not so smooth off the set. He and his wife, Lynn, learned their daughter Cheryl had a drug problem. Cheryl had been in a car accident in college. After the accident, she took drugs to ease her pain. She became addicted to the drugs.

The Landons sent Cheryl to a special place to get over her addiction. Michael Landon began speaking out against drug abuse. Former First Lady Nancy Reagan recruited him for her anti-drug campaign.

Landon also tackled another issue that concerned him. In 1976, he directed a movie he had written called *The Loneliest Runner*. It was about a boy who wet the bed. The movie told children not to be ashamed if they wet the bed. Landon didn't want other children to experience the pain he had.

All this time, Landon brought *Little House* to millions of viewers each week. He also worked behind the scenes to develop a new series for NBC in 1981. It was called *Father Murphy*. The series was about a 1870s gold prospector who pretends to be a priest to save a group of orphans.

Nancy Reagan with Michael Landon, as he makes an anti-drug speech.

Landon's hectic schedule began to drive a wedge between him and his wife. Rumors flew Landon was seeing other women. On talk shows, he insisted everything was fine. Finally, the couple separated and then divorced in 1982. Both suffered the pain of the divorce. Landon also felt the anger of his four children by Lynn.

To escape the pain, Landon jumped on an offer to star in a TV movie. He traveled to Thailand to film *Love is Forever*. It was the story of a journalist who risked death to rescue his fiancee in Laos. He arrived with his girlfriend, Cindy Clerico.

Filming was difficult. Landon was used to calling the shots. His word was law on the sets of *Little House* and even *Bonanza*. Landon often argued with the movie's director, Hall Bartlett. Bartlett edited the movie in secret to escape Landon's complaining. The movie turned out well, but not in Landon's eyes. He felt if he could not play a bigger part in it, it wouldn't be worthwhile.

ANGEL ON MY SHOULDER

Landon wanted to forget the troubles of *Love is Forever.*He began brainstorming a new TV series once *Little House* ended. He also married his girlfriend, Cindy. A few months later, he and Cindy had baby daughter Jennifer.

When Landon's daughter Cheryl was nearly killed in a car accident, Landon made a vow. He promised God that if He would let Cheryl live, Landon would create a TV show to help people. His new show would be about an angel that helped people.

The people at NBC were not sure about Landon's idea. They didn't know if anyone would want to watch a show about an angel. But Landon had two hit shows to his credit. NBC decided to give it a try. *Highway to Heaven* was born in 1984.

Landon continued his practical jokes, even as an angel. Once on the *Highway to Heaven* set he became very angry. He threw a piece of expensive camera equipment on the ground and smashed it. The camera operator was furious. Later the operator discovered the broken piece was a prop. Landon made it so he could pretend to break it.

Landon played angel Jonathon Smith for four years. The show became a favorite. It also showed people how they could help one another.

CRUSADING OFF THE SET

Many of Landon's TV shows and movies had messages of hope. Others called attention to problems such as the environment, bed wetting and drug abuse. Landon believed television could make life better for everyone.

Landon worked to make a difference off the TV set as well. He did a public service announcement for a new group, "Women Against Rape," in his hometown in New Jersey. His message was so popular the group spread across the nation.

He also believed in helping children with Down's syndrome. (Down's syndrome is a disability which cannot be treated or cured.) One of Landon's crew members, John Warren, had a child with Down's syndrome. Sometimes Warren asked Landon to visit with parents of other Down's syndrome children.

"We'd be in some city," Warren remembered. "When the mayor or local station owner invited us to dinner, Mike would often beg off. Then he'd invite some couple who asked for an autograph to join us, and we'd end up having dinner with strangers instead of VIPs. (Very important people.) That's the way he liked it."

Even on the set, Landon always had time for sick children. He worked with organizations that help dying children get their last wishes. Many sick children wanted to visit the "angel" from *Highway to Heaven*. Landon was always ready to talk with them.

FINAL PROJECT

For three years after *Highway to Heaven* finished, Landon worked on a variety of projects for NBC. He had more time to enjoy his family. Now he and Cindy also had a son, Sean.

In 1991, Landon began work on another television show called *US*. It would be about three generations of a family. Unfortunately, Landon never saw his project finished.

On April 8, 1991, Landon told the world he had cancer. He vowed to fight the often-fatal disease. "If I'm gonna die, death's gonna have to do a lot of fighting to get me," he said.

Landon refused to surrender his sense of humor to cancer. A friend asked him what he would do if he lost his hair while being treated for the cancer. Landon said, "I'm rich. I'll buy a hat." But no amount of fighting or joking could keep the disease at bay. Landon died July 1, 1991.

Millions of people were sad to lose such a talented performer. Even former President Ronald Reagan took note. "His tragic battle with cancer touched the hearts of every American," Reagan said. "As did his indomitable spirit."

People will always remember Landon for his love of family. He insisted on producing programs for the entire family. He refused to resort to violence to attract viewers. His shows carried strong messages of love, communication and cooperation.

Michael Landon with family in 1974: (from left) wife, Lynn; son, Michael Jr.; daughter, Shawna Leigh; daughter, Leslie Ann.

In September 1991, NBC broadcast the pilot movie of *US*. Sadly, there could be no television series to follow. Yet Landon fans can still see him in rebroadcasts of *Bonanza*, *Little House on the Prairie* and *Highway to Heaven*. Thanks to years of hard work and dedication, his spirit lives on.

Michael Landon waves to the media after leaving the hospital for a check-up.